To

_____

FROM

_____

ON THE OCCASION OF

_____

A KEEPSAKE JOURNAL FOR THE ONE YOU LOVE

My Daughter's

Blessing Book

WATERBROOK
PRESS

MY DAUGHTER'S BLESSING BOOK
PUBLISHED BY WATERBROOK PRESS
2375 Telstar Drive, Suite 160
Colorado Springs, Colorado 80920
A division of Random House, Inc.

ISBN 1-57856-432-8

Printed in the United States of America
2001—First Edition

10 9 8 7 6 5 4 3 2 1

The LORD bless you
  and keep you;
the LORD make his face shine upon you
  and be gracious to you;
the LORD turn his face toward you
  and give you peace.

NUMBERS 6:24-26

INTRODUCTION

*T*iny feet and big smiles.

Baby dolls and frilly dresses.

Snuggle hugs and sweet kisses.

Best friends and moody days.

First dates and broken hearts.

Victories and dreamy eyes.

Spreading wings and soaring heights.

We watch our daughter grow. We marvel at her uniqueness, her gifts, her God-given bent. We equip her. We teach her. We love her.

We look for ways to bless her.

We want her to arrive at womanhood knowing a few things. She is loved. She is beautiful. She possesses purpose. She is called by God.

On some days we are better at telling her these things than on others. Some days we forget, or we communicate a contradictory idea. Some days she seems blind to the truth about her life, her identity in Christ, her hope for the future. On such days our hearts threaten to stop, and we wonder,

Have I done enough?

She will probably never know the depths and tears and joys of our prayers for her as the Lord graces us through our parenting years. No matter. At every age and stage of her life—from birth to womanhood, perhaps to marriage and motherhood, and even beyond—we will continue seeking ways to give her some kind of tangible assurance, some testament of our love and God's as it applies to the details of her existence, some kind of personalized record. Whatever might happen to us, whatever route her life might take, she would always have it. She would always be able to read it, always be encouraged by it, ever pointed back, as if by a compass, to the love of Christ and her Father's perfect Word.

This is that record.

Or rather, this will become that record, just as soon as you put your pen to its paper.

How to Use This Book

Your daughter's *Blessing Book* contains twenty-one sets of pages for entries, each of which is introduced by a scripture. Ultimately, *you* get to decide when and how you want to complete this book for your daughter. Its flexible format offers several options, a few of which are listed on the following pages.

Pick a realistic approach that suits your desires, abilities, and circumstances. Keep your goals simple. Blessing your daughter doesn't have to be a flamboyant or spectacular gesture. In fact, the simplest words and briefest messages are often the most meaningful.

Here are some ideas—you may decide to use them all, just a few, or others of your own—to help you in the process:

WHEN SHOULD I WRITE?

One simple option is to write a once-a-year letter to your daughter on a meaningful annual date, such as her birthday, her "conversion birthday," a holiday, or the first day of each school year. You might give the journal to her each year to keep, taking it back only to write the next entry, or you might wait until she is of a certain age or has entered a particular rite of passage before giving the completed *Blessing Book* to her.

You might decide to write at shorter intervals: weekly, monthly, even daily during a period of time when she especially needs your encouragement. Your entries could be even less ordered than that if you prefer spontaneity. Allow them to be triggered by random events, such as an achievement, a time shared together, a new stage of life, a loss or disappointment, and so on.

Between entries, as you have thoughts but don't have time to write them down in a formal entry, jot short notes in the pages at the back of the *Blessing Book* to remind yourself of what you want to write. Use sticky notes if you run out of space.

WHAT SHOULD I SAY?

Try to keep the content of your entries focused on your daughter. You might:

♥ Affirm her uniqueness and giftedness, her talents and abilities.
♥ Reiterate your unconditional love for her.
♥ Share your hopes and dreams for her.

- ♥ Praise specific accomplishments, as well as her growth and maturity.
- ♥ Point her to the wisdom of God's Word as she seeks guidance for life.
- ♥ Identify a favorite scripture and explain its relevance to her life as you see it.
- ♥ Reflect upon the hope and promises contained in one or more of the scriptures in this *Blessing Book.*
- ♥ Applaud her efforts to live uprightly.
- ♥ Ask forgiveness for an error you've made in parenting her.
- ♥ Thank her for specific ways in which she has blessed you.
- ♥ Tell stories of events that occurred when she was too young to remember.
- ♥ Document events that she will want to remember later and explain why you think they're important.
- ♥ Make a list of her traits that you find commendable and praise what is beautiful in her.
- ♥ Encourage her during difficult times of trial, grief, disappointment, or waywardness.
- ♥ Identify life lessons you've learned and how they have shaped the way you parent her.
- ♥ Explain her special place in the family and describe what she contributes to it.
- ♥ Recount a special moment you shared with her and explain why you'll never forget it.

If you like, experiment with formats that lend variety to your entries:

- ♥ Write down your prayers for her.
- ♥ Craft a poem or song for your daughter, perhaps one easy for her to memorize.
- ♥ Retell a favorite story of blessing (or create a new one) with your daughter as the star.
- ♥ Paste favorite photos into the entry pages. Write captions that tell "the rest of the story."
- ♥ Press flowers that represent a special place or moment—her birthplace, favorite spot, first date, and so on—between the pages.
- ♥ Draw a picture that communicates a thought of blessing to her.

Moms and dads each play a unique role in blessing their daughters. Consider taking turns so that your daughter's *Blessing Book* contains words of love from both of you.

No matter how you decide to fill out this book or how long it takes you to complete it, the resulting blessing to your daughter will be immeasurable in the years to come. There are some things that only a parent can say, some holes only a parent can fill, some blessings only a parent can give. As you bless your daughter with the love of our Lord and Savior, he will bless you richly in return.

For Thou didst form my inward parts;
Thou didst weave me in my mother's womb.
I will give thanks to Thee, for I am fearfully
      and wonderfully made;
Wonderful are Thy works,
And my soul knows it very well.
My frame was not hidden from Thee,
When I was made in secret,
And skillfully wrought in the depths of the earth.
Thine eyes have seen my unformed substance;
And in Thy book they were all written,
The days that were ordained for me,
When as yet there was not one of them.

PSALM 139:13-16 (NASB)

*In all my prayers for all of you, I always pray with
joy…being confident of this, that he who began a
good work in you will carry it on to completion until
the day of Christ Jesus…. And this is my prayer: that
your love may abound more and more in knowledge
and depth of insight, so that you may be able to dis-
cern what is best and may be pure and blameless
until the day of Christ, filled with the fruit of righteousness that comes through Jesus Christ—to the glory
and praise of God.*

PHILIPPIANS 1:4,6,9-11

DATE: _____

Charm is deceptive, and beauty is fleeting;
*   but a woman who fears the L*ORD *is to be praised.*
Give her the reward she has earned,
*   and let her works bring her praise at the city gate.*

PROVERBS 31:30-31

May the LORD answer you when you are in distress;
*   may the name of the God of Jacob protect you.*
May he send you help from the sanctuary
*   and grant you support from Zion.*
May he remember all your sacrifices
*   and accept your burnt offerings.*
May he give you the desire of your heart
*   and make all your plans succeed.*
We will shout for joy when you are victorious
*   and will lift up our banners in the name of our God.*
May the LORD grant all your requests.

PSALM 20:1-5

People were bringing little children to Jesus to have him touch them, but the disciples rebuked them. When Jesus saw this, he was indignant. He said to them, "Let the little children come to me, and do not hinder them, for the kingdom of God belongs to such as these. I tell you the truth, anyone who will not receive the kingdom of God like a little child will never enter it." And he took the children in his arms, put his hands on them and blessed them.

MARK 10:13-16

[W]e have all had human fathers who disciplined us and we respected them for it. How much more should we submit to the Father of our spirits and live! Our fathers disciplined us for a little while as they thought best; but God disciplines us for our good, that we may share in his holiness. No discipline seems pleasant at the time, but painful. Later on, however, it produces a harvest of righteousness and peace for those who have been trained by it.

HEBREWS 12:9-11

Indeed, none of those who wait for Thee will be ashamed;
Those who deal treacherously without cause will be ashamed.
Make me know Thy ways, O LORD;
Teach me Thy paths.
Lead me in Thy truth and teach me,
For Thou art the God of my salvation;
For Thee I wait all the day.
Remember, O LORD, Thy compassion and Thy lovingkindnesses,
For they have been from of old.
Do not remember the sins of my youth or my transgressions;
According to Thy lovingkindness remember Thou me,
For Thy goodness' sake, O LORD.

PSALM 25:3-7 (NASB)

DATE: _____

Don't let anyone look down on you because you are young, but set an example for the believers in speech, in life, in love, in faith and in purity.... Watch your life and doctrine closely. Persevere in them, because if you do, you will save both yourself and your hearers.

1 TIMOTHY 4:12,16

*Your beauty should not come from outward adorn-
ment, such as braided hair and the wearing of gold
jewelry and fine clothes. Instead, it should be that of
your inner self, the unfading beauty of a gentle and
quiet spirit, which is of great worth in God's sight.
For this is the way the holy women of the past who put
their hope in God used to make themselves beautiful.*

1 PETER 3:3-5

For this reason, I bow my knees before the Father,
from whom every family in heaven and on earth
derives its name, that He would grant you, according
to the riches of His glory, to be strengthened with
power through His Spirit in the inner man; so that
Christ may dwell in your hearts through faith; and
that you, being rooted and grounded in love, may be
able to comprehend with all the saints what is the
breadth and length and height and depth, and to
know the love of Christ which surpasses knowledge,
that you may be filled up to all the fulness of God.

EPHESIANS 3:14-19 (NASB)

Blessed are the poor in spirit,
for theirs is the kingdom of heaven.
Blessed are those who mourn,
for they will be comforted.
Blessed are the meek,
for they will inherit the earth.
Blessed are those who hunger and thirst for righteousness,
for they will be filled.
Blessed are the merciful,
for they will be shown mercy.
Blessed are the pure in heart,
for they will see God.
Blessed are the peacemakers,
for they will be called sons of God.
Blessed are those who are persecuted because of righteousness,
for theirs is the kingdom of heaven.

MATTHEW 5:3-10

*Trust in the L*ORD *and do good;*
    dwell in the land and enjoy safe pasture.
*Delight yourself in the L*ORD
    and he will give you the desires of your heart.
*Commit your way to the L*ORD*;*
    trust in him and he will do this:
He will make your righteousness shine like the dawn,
    the justice of your cause like the noonday sun.

PSALM 37:3-6

But because of his great love for us, God, who is rich in mercy, made us alive with Christ even when we were dead in transgressions—it is by grace you have been saved. And God raised us up with Christ and seated us with him in the heavenly realms in Christ Jesus, in order that in the coming ages he might show the incomparable riches of his grace, expressed in his kindness to us in Christ Jesus. For it is by grace you have been saved, through faith—and this not from yourselves, it is the gift of God—not by works, so that no one can boast. For we are God's workmanship, created in Christ Jesus to do good works, which God prepared in advance for us to do.

EPHESIANS 2:4-10

If you make the L<small>ORD</small> your refuge,
  if you make the Most High your shelter,
no evil will conquer you;
  no plague will come near your dwelling.
For he orders his angels
  to protect you wherever you go.
They will hold you with their hands
  to keep you from striking your foot on a stone.
You will trample down lions and poisonous snakes;
  you will crush fierce lions and serpents under your feet!
The L<small>ORD</small> says, "I will rescue those who love me.
  I will protect those who trust in my name.
When they call on me, I will answer;
  I will be with them in trouble.
  I will rescue them and honor them.
I will satisfy them with a long life
  and give them my salvation."

<small>P<small>SALM</small> 91:9-16 (<small>NLT</small>)</small>

That is why we have a great High Priest who has gone to heaven, Jesus the Son of God. Let us cling to him and never stop trusting him. This High Priest of ours understands our weaknesses, for he faced all of the same temptations we do, yet he did not sin. So let us come boldly to the throne of our gracious God. There we will receive his mercy, and we will find grace to help us when we need it.

HEBREWS 4:14-16 (NLT)

*For the L*ORD *God is a sun and shield;*
*The L*ORD *gives grace and glory;*
No good thing does He withhold
    from those who walk uprightly.

PSALM 84:11 (NASB)

LORD, who may dwell in your sanctuary?
　　Who may live on your holy hill?
He whose walk is blameless
　　and who does what is righteous,
who speaks the truth from his heart
　　and has no slander on his tongue,
who does his neighbor no wrong
　　and casts no slur on his fellowman,
who despises a vile man
　　but honors those who fear the LORD,
who keeps his oath
　　even when it hurts,
who lends his money without usury
　　and does not accept a bribe against the innocent.
He who does these things
　　will never be shaken.

PSALM 15

The eyes of the LORD are on the righteous
and his ears are attentive to their cry;...
The righteous cry out, and the LORD hears them;
he delivers them from all their troubles.
The LORD is close to the brokenhearted
and saves those who are crushed in spirit.

PSALM 34:15,17-18

Therefore we do not lose heart. Though outwardly we are wasting away, yet inwardly we are being renewed day by day. For our light and momentary troubles are achieving for us an eternal glory that far outweighs them all. So we fix our eyes not on what is seen, but on what is unseen. For what is seen is temporary, but what is unseen is eternal.

2 CORINTHIANS 4:16-18

So we have continued praying for you ever since we first heard about you. We ask God to give you a complete understanding of what he wants to do in your lives, and we ask him to make you wise with spiritual wisdom. Then the way you live will always honor and please the Lord, and you will continually do good, kind things for others. All the while, you will learn to know God better and better. We also pray that you will be strengthened with his glorious power so that you will have all the patience and endurance you need. May you be filled with joy, always thanking the Father, who has enabled you to share the inheritance that belongs to God's holy people, who live in the light.

COLOSSIANS 1:9-12 (NLT)

May God himself, the God of peace, sanctify you through and through. May your whole spirit, soul and body be kept blameless at the coming of our Lord Jesus Christ. The one who calls you is faithful and he will do it.

1 THESSALONIANS 5:23-24

.